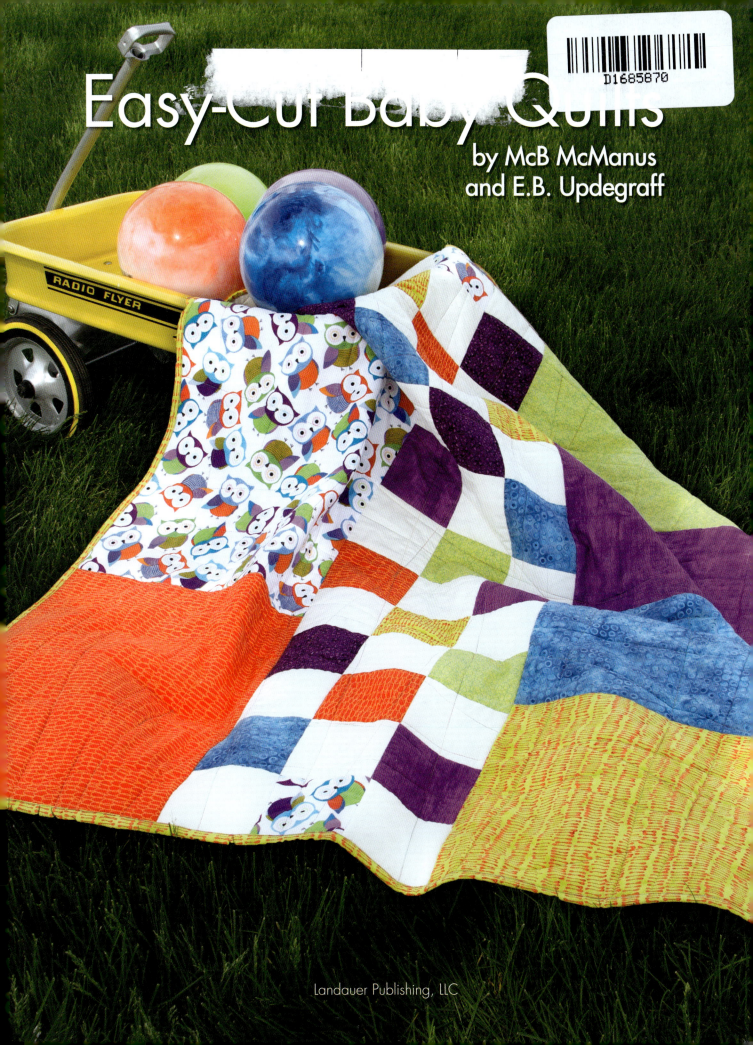

Easy-Cut Baby Quilts

by McB McManus
and E.B. Updegraff

Landauer Publishing, LLC

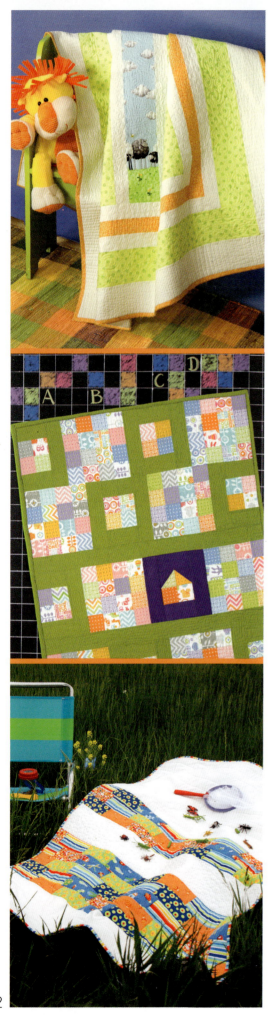

Easy-Cut Baby Quilts

Projects Copyright © 2015
by McB McManus and E.B. Updegraff

This book was designed, produced,
and published by Landauer Publishing, LLC
3100 101st Street, Urbandale, IA 50322
www.landauerpub.com
515/287/2144   800/557/2144

President/Publisher: Jeramy Lanigan Landauer
Vice President of Sales and Administration: Kitty Jacobson
Editor: Jeri Simon
Art Director: Laurel Albright
Photographer: Sue Voegtlin

ISBN 13: 978-1-935726-73-9
This book printed on acid-free paper.
Printed in United States
10-9-8-7-6-5-4-3-2-1

 FACEBOOK.COM/
LANDAUERPUBLISHING
 YOUTUBE.COM/
LANDAUERPUBLISHING
 PINTEREST.COM/
LANDAUERPUB

Table of Contents

Introduction

We all want to wrap a new baby in love...and what better way to do that than with a handmade quilt? We love giving quilts to our friends and family members as special gifts to mark the milestones in their lives, and a quilt welcoming a little one is a great way to start that tradition.

We are sure you'll find a pattern in this book to inspire you. The quilts are easy to cut and quick to stitch using pre-cut bundles or yardage cut to those familiar sizes.

Happy quilting,

McB & E.B.

Mod Baby Quilt

Finished quilt size approximately:

54" x 71"

Materials

1/2 yard orange print fabric

1-1/4 yards green print fabric

1/4 yard focus print fabric

1-3/4 yards white solid fabric

5-1/4 yards backing fabric

2/3 yard binding fabric

60" x 77" batting

wof = width of fabric
Fabric quantities based on 42"-44"-wide, 100% cotton fabrics

Cut the Fabrics

From orange print fabric, cut:

5—2-1/2" x wof strips

From green print fabric, cut:

8—5" x wof strips

From focus print fabric, cut:

1—5" x wof strip (fussy cut, if necessary)

From white solid fabric, cut:

12—2-1/2" x wof strips

6—5" x wof strips

From binding fabric, cut:

7—2-1/2" x wof strips

Assemble the Quilt Center

1 Lay out 5 white 2-1/2" x wof strips, 3 green print 5" x wof strips, and the 5" x wof focus print strip as shown.

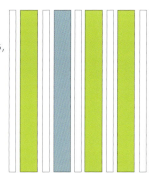

2 Sew the strips together. Press the seams in one direction to make a strip panel.

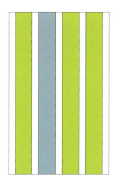

3 Square up the strip panel at the top and bottom.

4 Sew a 2-1/2" x wof white strip to the top and bottom of the strip panel. Trim any excess fabric to complete the quilt center.

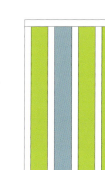

Add the Borders

Note: Refer to the Border Assembly Diagram when adding the borders.

1 Sew the 2-1/2" x wof orange strips together end-to-end to make one strip. Press seams open.

2 Measure the quilt center through the middle from top to bottom to determine the length of the quilt center. Cut 2 orange strips to this length. Sew the strips to the sides of the quilt center. Press seams toward the strips.

3 Measure the quilt center through the middle from side to side to determine the width of the quilt center. Include the side borders in the measurement. Cut 2 orange strips to this measurement. Sew the strips to the top and bottom of the quilt center. Press seams toward the strips.

4 Referring to steps 1-3 and the Border Assembly Diagram, sew the remaining 2-1/2" x wof white strips, 5" x wof green print strips and 5" x wof white strips to the quilt center. Press all seams toward the strips to complete the quilt top.

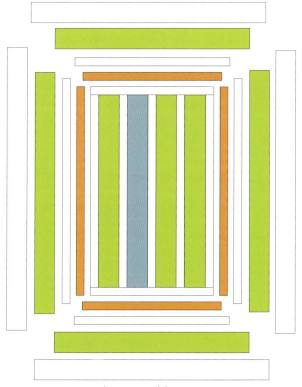

Border Assembly Diagram

Finish the Quilt

1. Layer the backing, batting, and quilt top. Baste the layers together and hand- or machine-quilt as desired.

2. Sew the 2-1/2"-wide binding strips together to make one continuous strip. Press the strip in half lengthwise, wrong sides together. Sew the binding to the front of the quilt, aligning the raw edges. Turn the binding over the edge to the back of the quilt and hand- or machine-stitch in place.

Size Twist

GROWTH CHART: Make a growth chart using the center panel and white sashing strips. Embroider inch marks along the sides of the sashing strips.

Backing Twist

Use fabric remnants from the quilt front to create an interesting quilt back.

Color Block Quilt

Finished quilt size approximately:

53" x 59"

Materials

7 half-yard cuts in assorted prints

1/2 yard light solid fabric

3-1/2 yards backing fabric

1/2 yard binding fabric

59" x 65" batting

wof = width of fabric
Fabric quantities based on 42"-44"-wide, 100% cotton fabrics
Half-yard cut = 18" x wof

Cut the Fabrics

From assorted prints, cut a total of:
3—18" x 20" rectangles

4—15-1/2" x 22" rectangles

From remaining fabric, cut: 19—5" squares

From light solid fabric, cut:
3—5" x wof strips

From the strips, cut: 20—5" squares

From binding fabric, cut:
6—2-1/2" x wof strips

Assemble the Sections

1 Sew the 18" x 20" rectangles together along the short edges to make the left quilt section. Press seams open.

2 Sew the 15-1/2" x 22" rectangles together along the long edges to make the right quilt section. Press seams open.

3 Sew a light solid 5" square to opposite sides of a print 5" square. Press seams open to make an A segment. Make a total of 7 A segments.

Make 7 A segments

4 Sew a print 5" square to opposite sides of a light solid 5" square. Press seams open to make a B segment. Make a total of 6 B segments.

Make 6 B segments

5 Sew the A and B segments together, alternating the segments beginning with an A segment. Press seams open to make the center quilt section.

Assemble the Quilt

1 Referring to the Quilt Assembly Diagram on page 11, lay out the left, center, and right quilt sections.

2 Sew the left quilt section to the center quilt section. Press seams open.

3 Sew the right quilt section to the opposite side of the center quilt section. Press seams open to complete the quilt top.

Quilt Assembly Diagram

Finish the Quilt

1 Square up the quilt top edges.

2 Layer the backing, batting, and quilt top. Baste the layers together and hand- or machine-quilt as desired.

3 Sew the 2-1/2"-wide binding strips together to make one continuous strip. Press the strip in half lengthwise, wrong sides together. Sew the binding to the front of the quilt, aligning the raw edges. Turn the binding over the edge to the back of the quilt and hand- or machine-stitch in place.

1. For each block, sew together four 5" fabric squares as shown in Diagram A, starting and stopping 1/4" from the top and bottom edges and backstitching to secure the seam. Press seam allowances open.

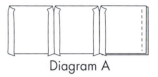

Diagram A

2. Sew together the remaining side edges of the first and fourth squares, starting and stopping 1/4" from the top and bottom edges.

3. Sew a 5" fabric square to the top edge of the block sides as shown in Diagram B. To make a sharp turn at the corners, leave the needle down in the fabric, lift the presser foot, and turn the fabric.

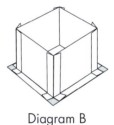

Diagram B

4. Sew a second square to the bottom edge of the block sides in the same manner, leaving one edge open for turning. Trim each corner as shown in Diagram C.

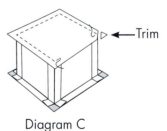

Diagram C

5. Turn the fabric block right side out. Tuck a foam cube into the fabric block through the opening. Whipstitch the opening closed.

Cornered Quilt

Finished quilt size approximately:

39" x 45"

Materials

2 fat eighths in assorted red prints

2 fat eighths in assorted aqua prints

1-3/4 yards light solid fabric

3 yards backing fabric

1/2 yard binding fabric

45" x 51" batting

wof = width of fabric
Fabric quantities based on 42-44"-wide, 100% cotton fabrics
Fat eighth = 9" x 22"

Cut the Fabrics

From one red print fat eighth, cut:
1—5" x wof strip
> From the strip, cut: 4—5" squares

From remaining red print fat eighth, cut:
1—5" x wof strip
> From the strip, cut: 2—5" squares

From one aqua print fat eighth, cut:
1—5" x wof strip
> From the strip, cut: 3—5" squares

From remaining aqua print fat eighth, cut:
1—5" x wof strip
> From the strip, cut: 2—5" squares

From light solid fabric, cut:
2—5" x wof strips
> From the strips, cut: 11—5" squares

6—4-1/2" x wof strips
> From the strips, cut:
> 1—4-1/2" x 35" rectangle
> 1—4-1/2" x 31" rectangle
> 1—4-1/2" x 27" rectangle
> 1—4-1/2" x 23" rectangle
> 1—4-1/2" x 19" rectangle
> 1—4-1/2" x 15" rectangle

1—21-1/2" x wof rectangle

From binding fabric, cut:
5—2-1/2" x wof strips

Assemble the Half-Square Triangles

1 Layer a 5" red print square on a 5" light solid square, right sides together.

2 Draw a diagonal line from corner to corner on the wrong side of the red print square. Sew a 1/4" on either side of the drawn line.

3 Cut on the drawn line. Press seam toward the red print fabric to make 2 half-square triangles. Square each unit to 4-1/2". Make a total of 12 red print half-square triangles.

Make 12

4 Referring to steps 1-3, make a total of 10 aqua print half-square triangles. You will use 9.

Make 10

Assemble the Rows

1 Referring to the diagram for half-square triangle placement and strip length, lay out the bottom 6 rows as shown.

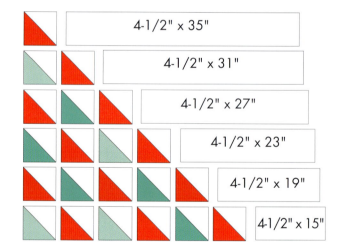

2 Sew the pieces in each row together. Press seams open.

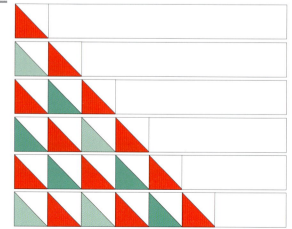

3   Sew the rows together, matching the half-square triangle seams in each row. Press the seams open to complete the bottom section of the quilt top.

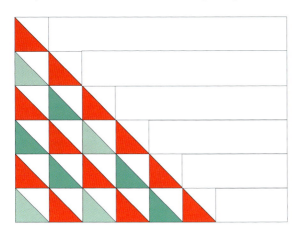

Assemble the Quilt Top

1   With right sides together, sew the light solid 21-1/2" x wof rectangle to the bottom section of the quilt top. Press seams open.

2   Trim the top section even with the bottom section to square up the quilt top.

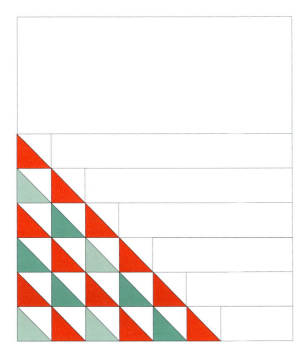

Finish the Quilt

1   Layer the backing, batting, and quilt top. Baste the layers together and hand- or machine-quilt as desired.

2   Sew the 2-1/2"-wide binding strips together to make one continuous strip. Press the strip in half lengthwise, wrong sides together. Sew the binding to the front of the quilt, aligning the raw edges. Turn the binding over the edge to the back of the quilt and hand- or machine-stitch in place.

Size Twist

Pillow

Make a pillow by sewing 9 half-square triangles together in 3 rows. Repeat to make the pillow back or use a solid piece of fabric. Approximate size: 12" x 12"

Little Schoolhouse Quilt

Finished quilt size approximately:

30" x 36"

Materials

41—5" assorted print squares OR
      1 Charm Pack with a minimum of 41 squares

3/4 yard green solid fabric

1 fat eighth purple solid fabric

1-1/4 yards backing fabric

1/3 yard binding fabric

34" x 40" batting

wof = width of fabric
Fabric quantities based on 42"-44"-wide, 100% cotton fabrics
Charm Pack = 5" squares

Cut the Fabrics

From assorted 5" print squares, cut:

159—2-1/2" squares

> Note: Cut each 5" square in half twice to get 4—2-1/2" squares.

1—3-3/8" square

From green solid fabric, cut:

6—2-1/2" x wof strips

> From 4 strips, cut:
> 14—2-1/2" x 4-1/2" rectangles
> 10—2-1/2" x 8-1/2" rectangles

Set the 2 remaining strips aside for sashing

From purple solid fabric, cut:

2—2-1/2" x 4-1/2" rectangles
2—2-1/2" x 8-1/2" rectangles
1—3-3/8" square

From binding fabric, cut:

4—2-1/2" x wof strips

Assemble the Blocks

Sixteen-Patch blocks

1   Lay out 16 assorted 2-1/2" print squares in 4 rows with 4 squares in each row as shown.

2   Sew the squares together in rows. Sew the rows together to complete the sixteen-patch block. Make a total of 8 sixteen-patch blocks.

Make 8

Four-Patch blocks

1   Lay out 4 assorted 2-1/2" print squares as shown. Sew the squares together to make a four-patch block. Make a total of 7 four-patch blocks.

Make 7

2   Sew 2-1/2" x 4-1/2" green solid rectangles to the top and bottom of the four-patch block.

3   Sew a 2-1/2" x 8-1/2" green solid rectangle to one side of the four-patch blocks. Set 4 of the blocks aside.

4   Sew 2-1/2" x 8-1/2" green solid rectangles to opposite sides of the 3 remaining four-patch blocks.

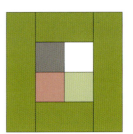

House block

Note: The featured quilt uses 2 different prints in the half-square triangles for a scrappier look. The instructions use 1 print.

1 Sew 2 assorted 2-1/2" print squares together as shown.

2 Layer the 3-3/8" print square on the 3-3/8" solid purple square, right sides together. Draw a diagonal line from corner to corner on the wrong side of the print square.

3 Sew a 1/4" on either side of the drawn line. Cut on the drawn line and press the pieces open to create 2 half-square triangles.

4 Sew the half-square triangles together as shown.

5 Sew the squares from step 1 and the half-square triangle set together as shown to make the block center.

6 Sew 2-1/2" x 4-1/2" purple solid rectangles to the top and bottom of the block center. Sew 2-1/2" x 8-1/2" purple solid rectangles to the remaining sides of the block center to complete the house block.

Size Twist

For charming, coordinated nursery décor make additional blocks and frame.

Assemble the Quilt

1 Referring to the Quilt Assembly Diagram, lay out the blocks and sashing strips as shown.

2 Sew the blocks together in rows. Sew the rows and sashing strips together to complete the quilt top.

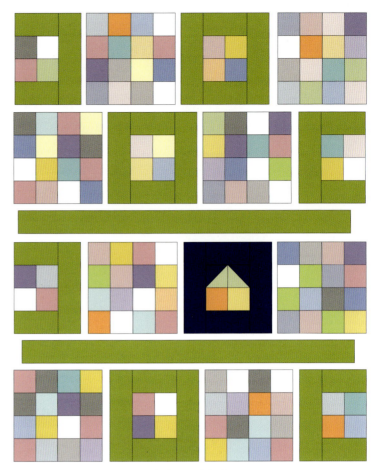

Quilt Assembly Diagam

Finish the Quilt

1 Square up the quilt top.

2 Layer the backing, batting, and quilt top. Baste the layers together and hand- or machine-quilt as desired.

3 Sew the 2-1/2"-wide binding strips together to make one continuous strip. Press the strip in half lengthwise, wrong sides together. Sew the binding to the front of the quilt, aligning the raw edges. Turn the binding over the edge to the back of the quilt and hand- or machine-stitch in place.

Size Twist

Sew 4 sixteen-patch blocks together to make a doll quilt.

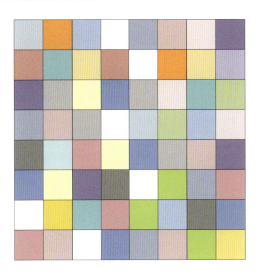

Referring to Assemble the Quilt Top on page 20, sew the two top or bottom rows together to make a play quilt.

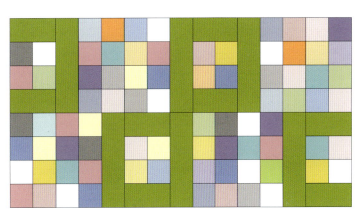

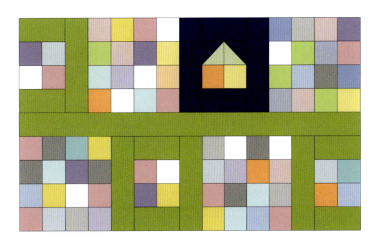

Moon and Stars Quilt

Finished quilt size approximately:

42" x 65"

Materials

2 yards gray print fabric

4 fat quarters in assorted white prints

1 fat quarter yellow print fabric

3-1/2 yards backing fabric

1/2 yard binding fabric

1-1/4 yards fusible web

50" x 73" batting

wof = width of fabric
Fabric quantities based on 42"-44"-wide, 100% cotton fabrics
Fat quarter = 18" x 22"

Cut the Fabric

Trim the gray print fabric to approximately 65" long.

From the binding fabric, cut:
6—2-1/2" x wof binding strips

Appliqué the Quilt

Note: The appliqué shapes have been reversed for you.

1 Trace the moon and star patterns on pages 26-27 onto the paper side of the fusible web. Trace the patterns in the numbers given.
1—Moon
5—Large Star
9—Medium Star
23—Small Star

Cut out the shapes leaving approximately 1/4" of web beyond the outside of each shape.

2 Fuse the moon shape onto the wrong side of the yellow print fabric. Fuse the star shapes to the wrong sides of the assorted white prints, following the manufacturer's instructions. Cut out the shapes on traced lines. Remove the paper backing from each shape.

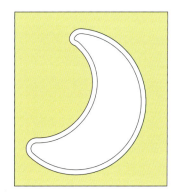

3 Referring to the Appliqué Placement Diagram, position the moon and stars onto the gray print. Fuse in place, following manufacturer's instructions.

Appliqué Placement Diagram

4 Using your favorite appliqué stitch, sew the moon and stars onto the gray print.

Finish the Quilt

1 Layer the backing, batting, and quilt top. Baste the layers together and hand- or machine-quilt as desired.

2 Sew the 2-1/2"-wide binding strips together to make one continuous strip. Press the strip in half lengthwise, wrong sides together. Sew the binding to the front of the quilt, aligning the raw edges. Turn the binding over the edge to the back of the quilt and hand- or machine-stitch in place.

Project Twist

MOBILE: Using two fabrics per shape, cut out the moon and star appliqué pieces. With right sides together, sew around the outside of the shapes leaving an opening for turning. Turn the shapes right side out and stuff with Poly-fil®. Stitch the opening closed. Hang the shapes with heavy thread or fishing wire from an embroidery hoop. Hang the moon in the center.

SOFT BLOCKS: Use the instructions above to make a variety of soft block toys.

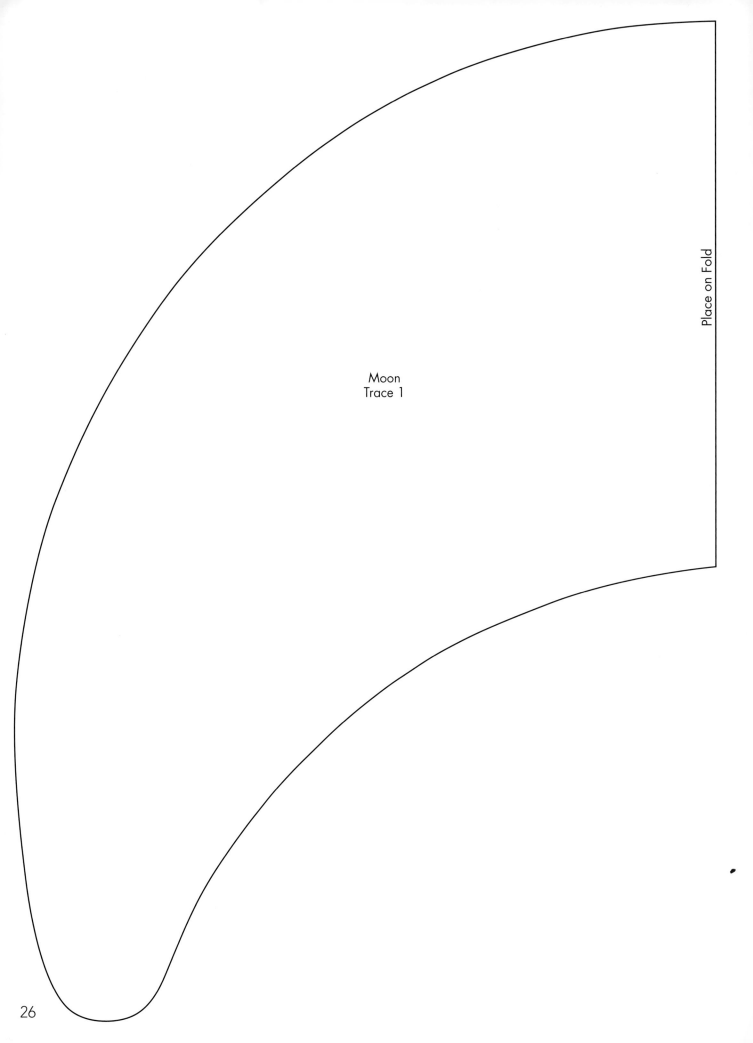

Moon
Trace 1

Place on Fold

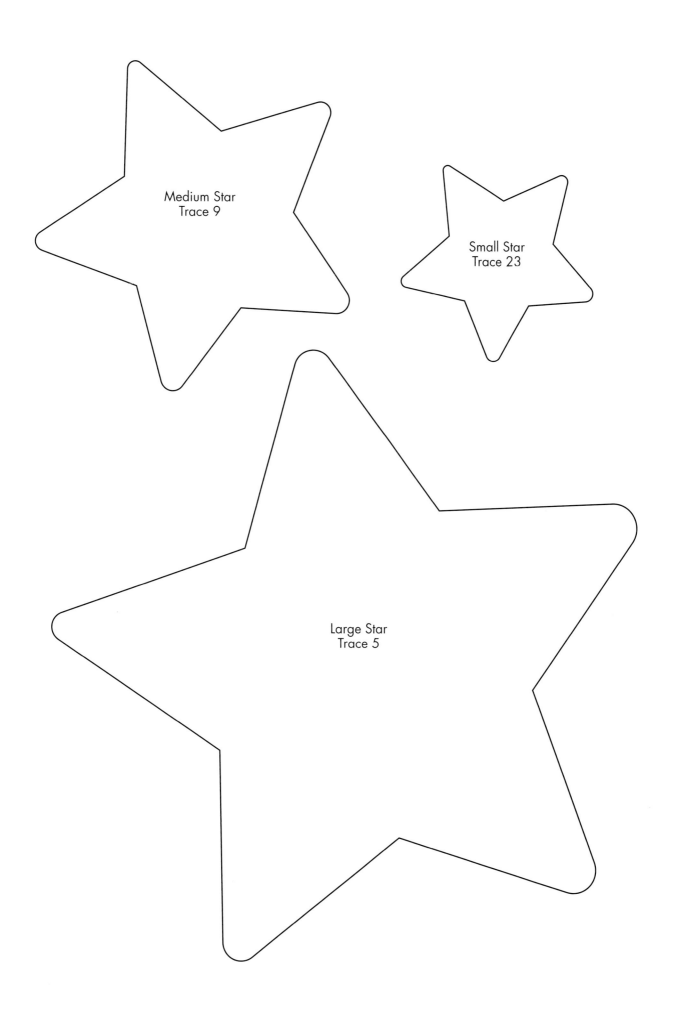

Medium Star
Trace 9

Small Star
Trace 23

Large Star
Trace 5

Hey Little Sister Quilt

Finished quilt size approximately:

52-3/4" x 60-1/2"

Pieced and quilted by Sue Voegtlin

Materials

1-3/4 yards pink print fabric

1-5/8 yards gray dot fabric

Fat eighth each light, medium and dark solid pink fabric

3-1/2 yards backing fabric

1/2 yard binding fabric

57" x 65" batting

wof = width of fabric
lof = length of fabric
Fabric quantities based on 42"-44"-wide, 100% cotton fabrics
Fat eighth = 9" x 22"

Cut the Fabrics

From pink print fabric, cut:

1—4-1/2" x lof strip

1—24-1/2" x lof strip

From gray dot fabric, cut:

1—24-1/2" x 36-1/2" strip

2—4-1/2" x wof strips

    From each strip, cut:

      1—4-1/2" x 24-1/2" strip

      1—4-1/2" x 16-1/2" strip

2—4-1/2" squares

4—5" squares

From *each* solid pink fat eighth, cut:

2— 4-1/2" squares

2—5" squares

From binding fabric, cut:

6—2-1/2" x wof strips

Assemble the Heart Block

1 Lay a 5" dark pink square on a gray dot square, right sides together.

2 Draw a diagonal from corner to corner on the wrong side of the top square. Sew a 1/4 " on either side of the drawn line.

3 Cut on the drawn line. Press seams open to make 2 dark pink/gray dot half-square triangles. Make a total of 4 dark pink/gray dot half-square triangles.

Make 4

4 Referring to steps 1-3, make a total of 4 light pink/gray dot half-square triangles and 2 medium pink/gray dot half-square triangles.

Note: You will only use 3 light pink/gray dot half-square triangles and one medium pink/gray dot half-square triangle.

Make 4   Make 2

5 Lay out the half-square triangles and 4-1/2" squares in rows as shown.

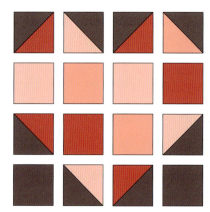

6 Sew the pieces together in rows.

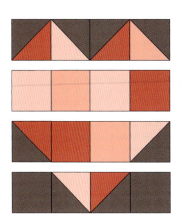

7 Sew the rows together to complete the heart block.

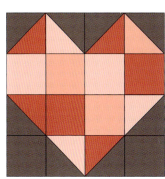

Assemble the Quilt

1 Sew the gray dot 4-1/2" x 16-1/2" strips to opposite sides of the heart block. Press.

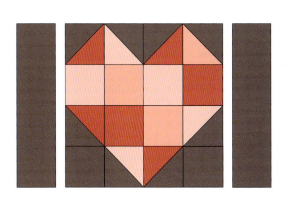

2 Sew the gray dot 4-1/2" x 24-1/2" strips to the remaining sides of the heart block. Press.

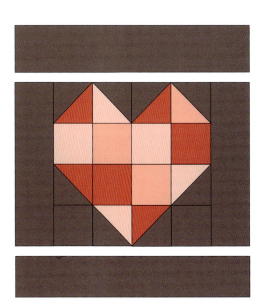

3 Sew the 24-1/2" x 36-1/2" gray dot strip to the top of the heart block to complete the heart panel. Press.

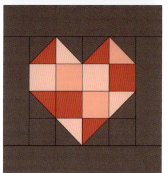

4 Referring to the Quilt Assembly Diagram, sew the pink print 4-1/2" x lof strip to the right side of the heart panel. Press.

5 Sew the pink print 24-1/2" x lof strip to the left side of the heart panel. Press.

6 Trim any excess fabric even with the heart panel.

Finish the Quilt

1 Layer the backing, batting, and quilt top. Baste the layers together and tie, hand- or machine-quilt as desired.

2 Sew the 2-1/2"-wide binding strips together to make one continuous strip. Press the strip in half lengthwise, wrong sides together. Sew the binding to the front of the quilt, aligning the raw edges. Turn the binding over the edge to the back of the quilt and hand- or machine-stitch in place.

Quilt Assembly Diagram

Quilting Twist

Combine different styles of quilting on the quilt top. The Hey Little Sister Quilt is stitched-in-the-ditch, tied and quilted with decorative machine stitches.

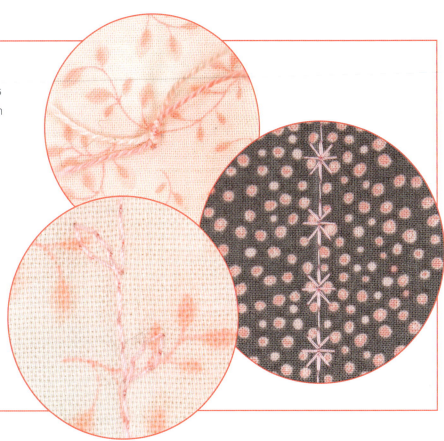

Color/Block Twist

Replace the heart block with a different block.

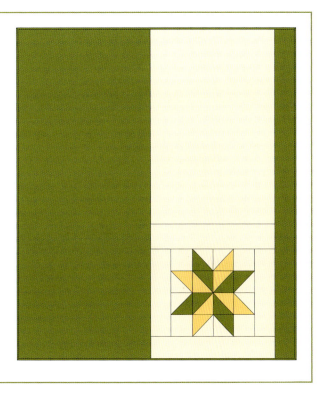

Sliding Scale Quilt

Finished quilt size approximately:

62-1/2" x 79-1/2"

Materials

40—2-1/2" x wof strips in assorted prints OR Jelly Roll bundle

2 yards gray solid fabric

5 yards backing fabric

2/3 yard binding fabric

69" x 86" batting

wof = width of fabric
Fabric quantities based on 42"-44"-wide, 100% cotton fabrics
Jelly Roll bundle = (40) 2-1/2" x wof strips

Cut the Fabrics

From gray solid fabric, cut:

25—2-1/2" x wof strips

From the strips, cut:

20—2-1/2" x 8" rectangles

20—2-1/2" x 15" rectangles

20—2-1/2" x 23" rectangles

From binding fabric, cut:

8—2-1/2" x wof strips

Assemble the Strip Panels

1 Separate the assorted 2-1/2" x wof print strips into 10 sets of 4 strips each.

2 Sew a 2-1/2" x 23" gray solid rectangle to one end of a print strip. Press the seams toward the gray strip to make an A strip set. Make 2 A strip sets.

Make 2 A

3 Sew a 2-1/2" x 8" gray solid rectangle to one end of a print strip. Sew a 2-1/2" x 15" rectangle to the opposite end of the print strip. Press seams toward the gray strips to make a B strip set. Make 2 B strip sets.

Make 2 B

4 Sew an A and B strip together along one long edge as shown. Press seams open to make a strip pair. Make 2 strip pairs.

Make 2 pairs

5 Sew strip pairs together as shown. Press seam open to make a strip panel. Make a total of 10 strip panels.

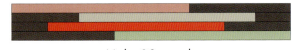

Make 10 panels

Assemble the Quilt

1 Referring to the Quilt Assembly Diagram, lay out the strip panels as shown.

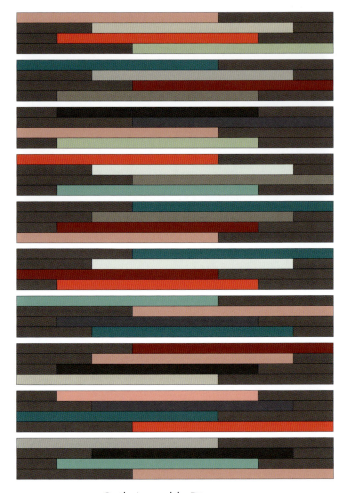

Quilt Assembly Diagram

2 Sew the strip panels together. Alternate the sewing direction with each panel. This will prevent the strip panels from becoming wavy while sewing. Press seams open.

3 Carefully trim the side edges to square up the quilt top.

Finish the Quilt

1 Layer the backing, batting, and quilt top. Baste the layers together and hand- or machine-quilt as desired.

2 Sew the 2-1/2"-wide binding strips together to make one continuous strip. Press the strip in half lengthwise, wrong sides together. Sew the binding to the front of the quilt, aligning the raw edges. Turn the binding over the edge to the back of the quilt and hand- or machine-stitch in place.

Size Twist

NAP BAG: Referring to page 36, sew 5 strip panels together. After layering, quilting and binding, fold the quilt in half lengthwise with right sides together. Sew the bottom of the folded quilt together. Measure the long open edge and cut a sew-on Velcro® strip to fit the opening. Sew the Velcro® strip in place. Approximate size: 31" x 40".

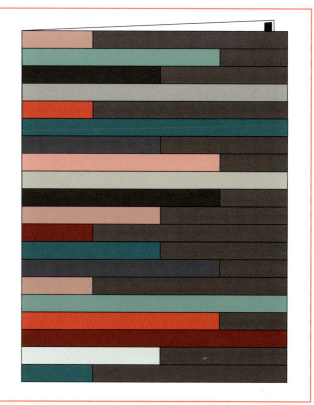

Tilted Quilt

Finished quilt size approximately:

39" x 62"

Materials

7 fat quarters in assorted prints

1-1/4 yards white solid fabric

3-3/4 yards backing fabric

1/2 yard binding fabric

45" x 68" batting

wof = width of fabric
Fabric quantities based on 42"-44"-wide, 100% cotton fabrics
Fat quarter = 18" x 22"

Cut the Fabrics

From each assorted print fat quarter, cut:

2—6" x wof strips.

 From each strip, cut: 5—3" x 6" rectangles

From binding fabric, cut:

6—2-1/2" x wof strips

Assemble the Strip Panels

1   Sew 8 assorted print 3" x 6" rectangles together along the short edges to make a strip. Press the seams in one direction. Make a total of 8 strips.

Make 8

2   Sew 3 strips together, offsetting each strip by approximately 1" to make strip panel A.

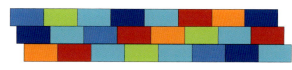

Make 1 A

3   Referring to step 2, sew 5 strips together, offsetting each strip by approximately 1" to make strip panel B.

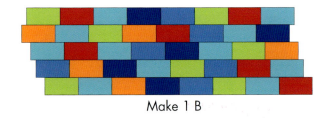

Make 1 B

Assemble the Quilt

1   Press the white solid fabric. Lay the fabric on a cutting surface and square up the edges.

2   Referring to the Cutting Diagram, measure, mark, and cut the white solid fabric as shown.

Note: Take special care not to stretch or distort the exposed bias edges.

3   Referring to the Quilt Assembly Diagram, lay out the white solid sections and the strip panels.

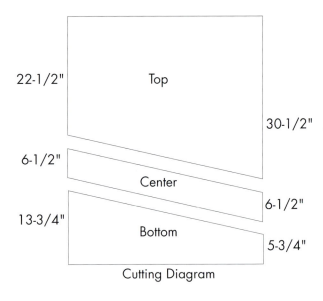

22-1/2"

30-1/2"

6-1/2"

13-3/4"

6-1/2"

5-3/4"

Top

Center

Bottom

Cutting Diagram

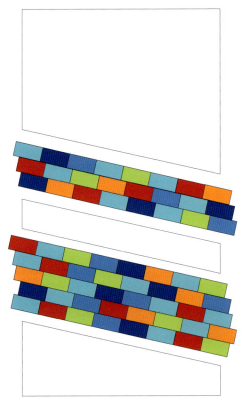

Quilt Assembly Diagram

4   Sew the top section to one long edge of strip panel A.

5   Sew the center section to the opposite long edge of strip panel A.

6 Sew one long edge of strip panel B to the opposite side of the center section.

7 Sew the bottom section to the opposite long edge of strip panel B to complete the quilt top.

8 Square up the quilt top edges.

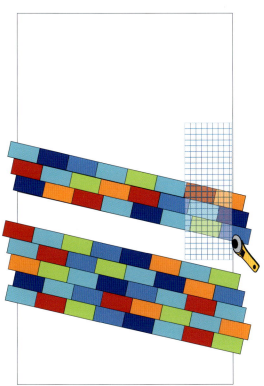

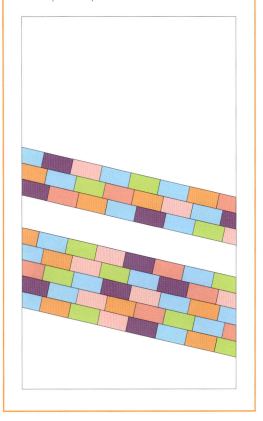

Color Twist

Pick soft solid hues for a cute and sophisicated twist on this pattern that still says 'baby'.

Finish the Quilt

1 Layer the backing, batting, and quilt top.
Baste the layers together and hand- or machine-quilt as desired.

2 Sew the 2-1/2"-wide binding strips together to make one continuous strip. Press the strip in half lengthwise, wrong sides together. Sew the binding to the front of the quilt, aligning the raw edges. Turn the binding over the edge to the back of the quilt and hand- or machine-stitch in place.

Space Quilt

Finished quilt size approximately:

34" x 42"

Materials

1/2 yard planet print fabric

1/2 yard star print fabric

1/2 yard red solid fabric

5/8 yard gray solid fabric

1-1/2 yards backing fabric

1/2 yard binding fabric

40" x 48" batting

wof = width of fabric
Fabric quantities based on 42"-44"-wide, 100% cotton fabrics

Cut the Fabrics

From planet print fabric, cut:

5—2-1/2" x wof strips

> From 1 strip, cut: 4—2-1/2" squares
> The remaining portion of the strip will
> be used in the blocks.

From star print fabric, cut:

5—2-1/2" x wof strips

From red solid fabric, cut:

5—2-1/2" x wof strips

From gray solid fabric, cut:

8—2-1/2" x wof strips

> From 1 strip, cut: 8—2-1/2" squares
> The remaining portion of the strip will
> be used in the blocks.

From binding fabric, cut:

5—2-1/2" x wof strips

Assemble the Courthouse Steps Blocks

1 Sew a 2-1/2" gray solid square to opposite sides of a 2-1/2" planet square. Press seams toward the gray squares to complete the block center.

2 Sew a 2-1/2" x wof red strip to the top and bottom of the block center. Press seams toward the red strips. Trim the strips even with the block center.

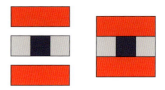

3 Sew a 2-1/2" x wof planet strip to opposite sides of the step 2 unit. Press seams toward the planet strips. Trim the strips.

4 Sew a 2-1/2" x wof star strip to the top and bottom of the step 3 unit. Press seams toward the star strips. Trim the strips.

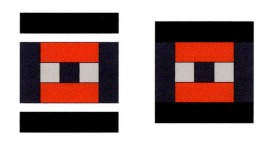

5 Referring to steps 1-4 and the Block Assembly Diagram, sew 2 additional rounds of strips to the step 4 unit. Always press the seams toward the outside strips to complete a Courthouse Steps block. Make a total of 4 Courthouse Steps blocks.

Block Assembly Diagram
Make 4

Cutting the Blocks

1 Referring to the Block Cutting Diagrams, cut 1 Courthouse Steps block in half vertically, cut 1 in half horizontally, and cut 1 into quarters. One block willl remain uncut

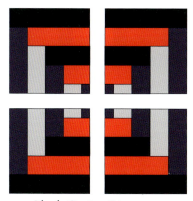

Block Cutting Diagrams

Assemble the Quilt

1 Referring to the Quilt Assembly Diagram, lay out the block pieces in rows as shown.

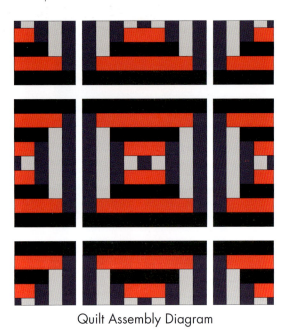

Quilt Assembly Diagram

2 Sew the pieces together in rows.

3 Sew a 2-1/2" x wof gray strip to the top and bottom of rows 1 and 3. Press the seams toward the gray strips.

4 Sew the rows together to complete the quilt top.

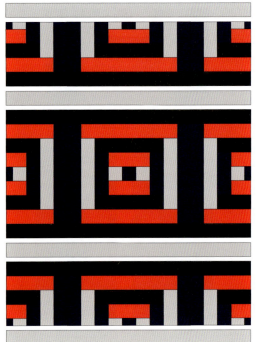

Finish the Quilt

1 Square up the quilt top edges.

2 Layer the backing, batting, and quilt top. Baste the layers together and hand- or machine-quilt as desired.

3 Sew the 2-1/2"-wide binding strips together to make one continuous strip. Press the strip in half lengthwise, wrong sides together. Sew the binding to the front of the quilt, aligning the raw edges. Turn the binding over the edge to the back of the quilt and hand- or machine-stitch in place.

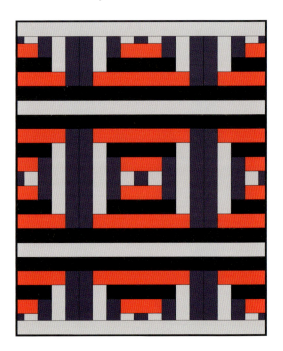

Size Twist

BURP CLOTHS: Back the half log cabin blocks with terrycloth to make burp cloths.

Quilting Twist

Quilt in a circular pattern to replicate the planets in the fabric.

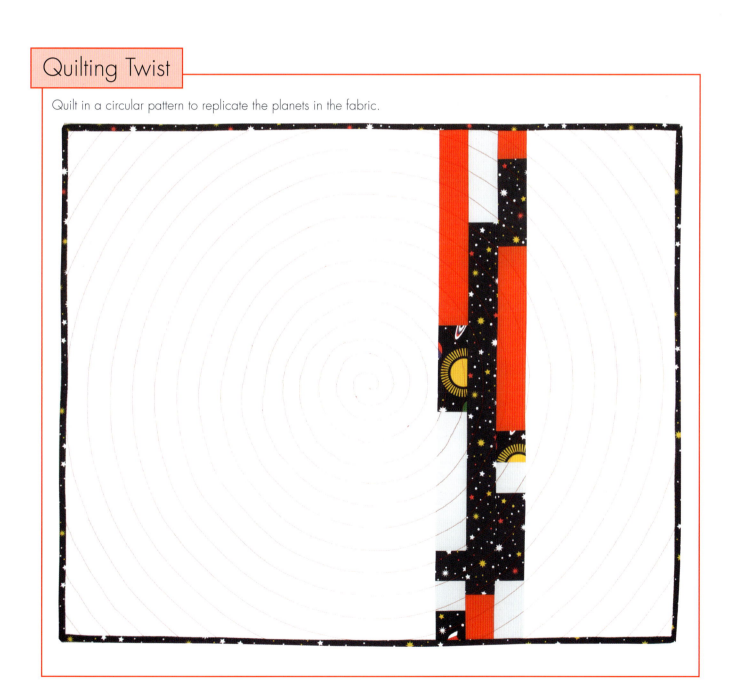

About the Authors

A quilting partnership started years ago when McB and E.B. met while working for Landauer Publishing. Together and separately, they have created quilts, tutorials and projects for the fans and followers of Landauer Publishing and for their friends, family and community. Through their friendship, they design quilts as a team: McB takes on the piecing, while E.B. does the quilting - they happily share the task of shopping for and selecting fabrics. McB and E.B. both live in Des Moines, Iowa.

McB   E.B.